HOW TO MAKE BATH BOMBS

A Beginner's Guide to Making Homemade Bath Bombs Step-By-Step

Legal & Disclaimer

The information contained in this book and its contents is not designed to replace or take the place of any form of medical or professional advice; and is not meant to replace the need for independent medical, financial, legal or other professional advice or services, as may be required. The content and information in this book has been provided for educational and entertainment purposes only.

The content and information contained in this book has been compiled from sources deemed reliable, and it is accurate to the best of the Author's knowledge, information, and belief. However, the Author cannot guarantee its accuracy and validity and cannot be held liable for any errors and/or omissions. Further, changes are periodically made to this book as and when needed. Where appropriate and/or necessary, you must consult a professional (including but not limited to your doctor, attorney, financial advisor or such other professional advisor) before using any of the suggested remedies, techniques, or information in this book.

Upon using the contents and information contained in this book, you agree to hold harmless the Author from and against any damages, costs, and expenses, including any legal fees potentially resulting from the application of any of the information provided by this book. This disclaimer applies to any loss, damages or injury caused by the use and application, whether directly or indirectly, of any advice or information presented, whether for breach of contract, tort, negligence, personal injury, criminal intent, or under any other cause of action.

You agree to accept all risks of using the information presented in this book.

You agree that by continuing to read this book, where appropriate and/or necessary, you shall consult a professional (including but not limited to your doctor, attorney, or financial advisor or such other advisor as needed) before using any of the suggested remedies, techniques, or information in this book.

and everything else that you are taking away from this book. :)

I purposefully tried to write this book so that anybody can understand it, not just people who are already in the new age/spirituality/self-help conversation. So I trust if you are guided to share it with someone, the message will reach them in a way that works for their life.

But believe it or not, the most important thing you can do is not give this book to a friend. The most important thing you can do is just bring your presence to every relationship, every environment, and every space which is currently a part of your life.

When are show up with a powerful understanding of your unique identity, people notice. It might sound like a paradox, but I can tell you from experience. People will be able to tell, and in a beautiful mystical way, it will make them want to discover themselves.

When you show up from a place of self-acceptance, people can tell. And although it might initially confuse, even irritate them, when shame no longer works on you, eventually they will desire the freedom you live in every day.

And when you start being yourself, not copying a trend that changes it up a little, but really bringing your true self into every single moment, everybody in your life will get the message. You are a person that knows how to find yourself, love yourself, and be yourself. And that is possible for them too, because that is possible for all of us.

Trust this truth, friends. Your presence is the change agent. I believe in you and the change that the universe is feeling right now because you are here.

When you show up as yourself, it's better for all of us.

Thank you, beloved.

Table of Contents

Introduction

There's something about bath bombs that make baths magical and fun, best described as fireworks for your bath. Once you drop a bath bomb into the tub, it starts to fizz and bubble with different scents and colors. Some may have flower petals in them while others are just plain, but they will all make you feel and smell good.

Bath bombs are all the rage these days. Just go to any website selling soap and you'll see them plastered everywhere. While they make great gift items and there are plenty of different brands you can grab on the shelves of your local grocery store, wouldn't it be nice to make your own?

There are many benefits to making your own bath bombs, but the biggest reason is that you know what goes into them so you can ensure that all the ingredients and materials used are safe. There have been issues in the past with some commercial bath bombs being made from toxic ingredients. The skin is such a porous organ that it allows all kinds of materials—chemicals and all—to be absorbed into the body. That's why making your own bath bombs is a great way to enjoy your bath time and ensure your safety. Let this book serve as your guide to making your own bath bombs.

Bath Bomb Basics

Bath bombs are for everyone. They are not only for children, but adults too. Imagine a small ball fizzing wildly in your bath water and emitting all sorts of colors and scents. Before you make any bath bombs, it is important that you learn about the basics.

Advantages of Making Your Bath Bombs

Buying bath bombs is easy and you can find them anywhere from online stores to local supermarkets. However, there are many advantages to making your own bath bombs. Aside from ensuring that you only use safe ingredients, listed below are other benefits of making your own bath bombs:

- **Save money:** Commercial bath bombs can be pricey and if you are addicted to using them during your bath time, wouldn't it be more beneficial to make your own? The money you will save from making your own bath bombs can be used to fund more important things.

- **Customize your own bath bombs:** The problem with buying bath bombs is that you might not be able to find the ones you really want. Making your own gives you the freedom to customize your bath. You can create them from a variety of ingredients and scents so that you can use a different kind every week.

- **Know what you are getting:** If you are allergic to some ingredients, making your own bath bombs is a great way to ensure that you know what you are getting and avoid triggering any allergic reactions.

- **Great gift ideas:** Bath bombs are great gift ideas that you can give to your friends and family. You can even customize them depending on the recipients of your gifts.

Uses of Bath Bombs

Most people think that bath bombs are only used to entertain people during their bath time. After all, they look like silly little balls that make bath time fun, but they have many benefits that anyone can enjoy. Below are the top uses of bath bombs to encourage you to make your own.

- **Skin conditioning:** Bath bombs contain ingredients that can soften or improve the condition of your skin. Some of these skin-rejuvenating ingredients include Vitamin E, coconut oil and tea tree oil.

- **Hair conditioning:** Who says bath bombs are only for the skin? If you want to wash your hair while soaking in the bath, bath bombs contain ingredients that will give your hair and scalp the care they need. Bath bombs containing ingredients like rosemary and thyme do wonders for the scalp, especially if you suffer from dandruff.

- **Stress relief:** Perhaps one of the most important benefits of using bath bombs is their calming effects. Ingredients such as lavender oil and Epsom salt can make you feel refreshed and relaxed.

- **Cold relief:** Soaking in a tub with bath bombs can help clear your sinuses when you have a cold. Bath bombs that contain essential oils such as eucalyptus can have beneficial effects to the body and the nose.

- **Sprains:** If you suffer from pain in your ligaments, then you must be suffering from a sprain. If your joints ache after an active and productive day, soaking in a tub with bath bombs can provide instant relief. Bath bombs that contain ingredients such as rosemary, peppermint and ginger have anti-inflammatory properties that can resolve aches and pains in the body.

- **Cleaners:** Did you know that when you place bath bombs into your bath water, they also clean the surface of the tub? Technically, baking soda is an industrial cleaner. So, the next time you use a bath bomb, remember that it is also doing good for your tub.

- **Perfect for pets:** Yes, bath bombs are also perfect for pets. They are natural cleaners and as long as they do not contain essential oils, they will not irritate your pet. So, ditch your commercial pet shampoo for a more natural pet cleaner.

Kinds of Bath Bombs

Bath bombs come in many forms and types with a wide variety of benefits. If you want to make your own bath bombs, it is important that you know the different types so you know which materials and ingredients you will need to make them.

- **Basic bath bomb:** This is made using simple ingredients that you can find at home-baking soda, citric acid, coloring and cornstarch.

- **Milky bath bombs:** This is made from milk with a combination of butter and other ingredients. The purpose of this bath bomb is to moisturize your skin as well as improve the quality of your skin. This bath bomb is perfect for people who suffer from dry skin.

- **Softening bath bombs:** As the name implies, this bath bomb can help soften your skin. It is often made with additional ingredients such as coconut oil, almond oil and shea butter to make your skin super soft after taking a bath. It is perfect for people who have severely flaky and dry skin.

- **Herbed or flowered bath bombs:** This type of bath bomb is made from typical basic bath bomb ingredients. The only difference is that it also contains dried herbs or flowers. These create a beautiful visual effect when they explode in bath water. However, your tub will get a little messy because they leave tiny pieces of herbs and flowers floating in the water. This type of bath bomb is great for a foot spa.

Equipment and Supplies

Bath bombs are hard-packed "balls" that are made from a mixture of dry ingredients that react to water. They form effervescence; this is where the name "bath bomb" comes from. Making bath bombs is part craft and part science. The materials are very simple and can often be found in the kitchen or can be bought in your local grocery store. This chapter is dedicated to the discussion of the materials, equipment and ingredients used to make bath bombs.

Ingredients

The ingredients used to make bath bombs are very simple but they each serve an important function. It is crucial that you understand what these ingredients are so that you can understand their mechanics and make that perfect bath bomb. Listed below are the types of materials you will need.

Baking Soda

Baking soda is the most important ingredient when it comes to making bath bombs. It is a natural cleanser that comes with a lot of benefits for the skin. Baking soda has anti-bacterial and anti-inflammatory properties that can help improve the quality of inflamed skin such as acne. It also helps remove dead skin cells, leaving your skin softer and more even-toned. Furthermore, baking soda can neutralize an imbalance of your skin's pH level.

Epsom Salt

Epsom salt contains the mineral magnesium, which has a lot of health benefits. It can help relieve stress, ease muscle aches, soothe sunburn and replenish moisture in the skin. Moreover, magnesium is also found to have a relaxing effect on the body and can reduce the feeling of anxiety. The skin easily absorbs Epsom salt once it is dissolved in warm water since warm water opens the pores,

Citric Acid

Citric acid is what makes the bath bomb fizz and bubble up when in contact with water. It is an organic material that occurs naturally in fruits such as grapefruits, lemons and oranges. Aside from causing the bath bombs to fizz, it also helps loosen the damaged, outer layers of the skin to allow younger skin to replace it. It also helps fortify blood vessels just underneath the skin.

Cornstarch

Cornstarch or corn flour is a common ingredient in cosmetic formulations to control the viscosity and for its skin conditioning properties. When used in bath bombs, it helps control the chemical reaction between the baking soda, citric acid and water, thus providing a more luxurious effervescence. It is best to combine the baking soda and cornstarch before the citric acid is added to remove the pitting or cracking of the bath bomb.

Coloring

While not necessary, coloring can be added to bath bombs to make them look more attractive. Choose cosmetic grade dyes or pearlescent micas.

Epsom Salt

Epsom salt has a lot of benefits for the body. It can help relax sore muscles and cure skin maladies. It contains magnesium, which is important for the physiological functioning of the cells. If you don't have Epsom salt, other salts may be used such as pink sea salt and Dead Sea salt

Essential Oils

Essential oils can provide many health benefits. They are typically used for aromatherapy, but they can also be used to help improve skin quality. As there are a lot of essential oils you can use, you have the freedom to choose which ones you want in your bath bombs depending on the purpose you have in mind. For instance, you can use lavender or lemon oil for their calming effects.

Butters

Oils and butter such as sweet almond oil, shea butter and coconut oil can moisturize and hydrate your skin, leaving it soft and supple. Other kinds of butter you can use include avocado butter, cocoa butter, coffee butter and mango butter. Different oils come with different benefits. For instance, sweet almond oil is known for its ability to protect the skin against UV radiation damage.

Additives

There are many other additives you can use in your bath bombs. Your creativity is the limit when it comes to adding whatever your heart desires. Below are some examples of additives you can put in your bath bombs:

- *Dried flowers and herbs:* Dried flowers and herbs can make your bath bombs look more attractive. You can use whatever you have on hand.

- *Oatmeal:* Oatmeal can help exfoliate your skin and leave it feeling refreshed.

- *Witch hazel:* Witch hazel is added to help the bath bomb retain its solid shape. It also has astringent properties that help relieve inflammation on the skin, fade bruises faster and smooth out blemishes.

Materials

You are not required to purchase expensive materials and equipment to create your own bath bombs. In fact, you can use whatever materials you have at home. Once you start making bath bombs, it is important to make sure that you have dedicated equipment that is used only to make bath bombs and nothing else. Listed below is the equipment you will need to make these bath necessities.

- **Bowls for mixing:** Use either a stainless steel or glass bowl when mixing your ingredients as these materials will not react to the ingredients. Avoid using a copper bowl because it will react to baking soda. If glass and metal bowls are not available, you can use ceramic or plastic.

- **Wooden spoon or spatula:** Use a wooden spoon or spatula to mix all ingredients together. As much as possible, try to avoid handling the raw ingredients as the mixture might be too strong for your hands to handle.

- **Gloves:** There are times when you must use your hands to mix all ingredients. This is especially true if the mixture becomes too thick and your wooden spoon or spatula no longer works. Make sure you wear gloves when mixing with your hands to protect them from any possible reactions from the ingredients.

- **Spray bottle:** It is essential that you have a spray bottle full of water on standby so you can adjust the amount of moisture in the bath bomb. While some people prefer to dump water by the cup, using a spray bottle allows you to carefully add moisture into the mixture and make fewer mistakes.

- **Bath bomb molds:** You need molds to shape your bath bombs. While there are many online stores where you can buy molds, you can also be creative and use various materials such as empty egg trays, ice cube trays and many others.

Instructions

Making bath bombs is not rocket science. It does not require extensive skills. Different bath bombs are made using different processes, but this chapter will focus on the process of making basic bath bombs.

Prepare the Things You Need

The first thing you need to do is prepare everything that you need. For the sake of brevity, this section will not give accurate measurements of the ingredients needed as that will be discussed in detail in the succeeding chapters. The basic materials that you need to prepare are as follows:

- Citric acid

- Baking soda

- Cornstarch

- Water

- Vegetable or olive oil

- Food coloring (optional)

- Molds

It is also important to prepare your equipment, including mixing bowls, spatula and muffin trays. Everything must be ready before you start so you can work systematically and without interruption.

The Process of Making Bath Bombs Is Science

This process is not rocket science but it must be precise so the ingredients do not fizz up halfway through. This section will give you the basics and the details of why things are done the way they are. You must remember that everything has a reason. Below are the general steps to make bath bombs.

1. Measure Dry Ingredients

To make it easy, it is best to measure all the dry ingredients first. That way, you know that you have all the ingredients needed. This is helpful for absent-minded people. You can also skip this step and just dump everything into your mixing bowl.

2. Mix Dry Ingredients

It is crucial to mix the dry ingredients such as the citric acid, baking soda, cornstarch, Epsom salt and others in a mixing bowl. This is to ensure that the citric acid does not react with the baking soda and become activated when it encounters moisture.

The combination of a high pH powder (baking soda) and low pH powder (citric acid) is what creates the effervescence, or bubbles. It is important to note that the citric acid replaces vinegar and it reacts to the baking powder only in the presence of enough moisture or water.

I prefer to mix the ingredients with my hand so I can crumble all the balled up baking soda into finer granules.

3. Add Wet Ingredients

I like to add the wet ingredients in succession so I can make sure I have the right amount of wetness.

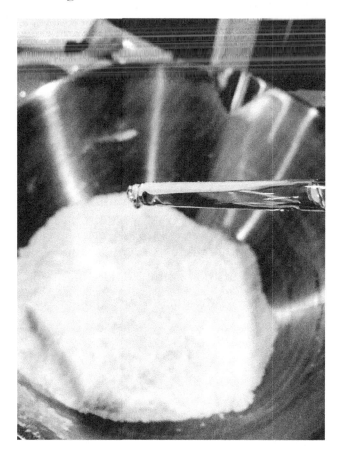

The first wet ingredient I add is the essential oil. I use as much as I need to create a pleasant aroma. After adding the oil, I mix it in with my hands.

The next wet ingredient I add is the coloring. Gel and liquid food coloring both work well. I suggest using a dropper to add a few drops at a time while mixing well after each addition so you get the color you want. Do not use too much food coloring if you don't want to get out of the bathtub looking like Smurfette! The photo on the right shows the mixture after I added food coloring.

The last wet ingredient I add is the oil. I choose oils that will not cause too much fizzing. Remember, if you add too much liquid at one time, fizzing occurs and then you will have a fizzled-out bath bomb. So, try to do this last step as slowly and surely as you can, especially when using water. If fizzing occurs, just press it down with the back of a spoon.

4. Stuff into Molds

Once you have mixed all ingredients, you should achieve a consistency like wet sand. Stuff the mixture into molds as soon as possible. You do not want the mixture to dry while still in the bowl. If the mixture dries, you may need to adjust the moisture content, which could result in more fizzing or your bath bombs no longer reacting to water.

For maximum efficiency, make sure you already have enough molds prepared. You don't need to buy fancy molds; you can use ice cube trays or other molds that you already have in your kitchen.

5. Let Them Air Dry

Once the mixture has been stuffed into molds, allow it to dry in the air. You might want to give it a full day or more to dry completely. Put the molds in a place that is not too humid. Avoid the kitchen counter or near the bathroom because the bath bombs will absorb moisture in the air. Once they are dry, pop them out and test them. If you live in a humid place, you might have to bake them in the oven for 45 minutes at 1500F to dry them effectively.

Once they're done drying, carefully remove your bath bombs from the molds.

6. Testing Bath Bombs

Before giving them to your friends and family, it is important to test the bath bombs. You don't need a bathtub full of water to do this. You can drop one or two of them in a small basin and observe how much they bubble.

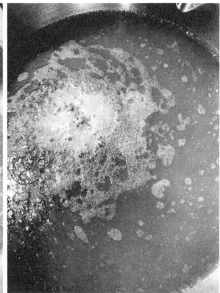

Molding Bath Bombs

Molding bath bombs give them the desired shape. While stuffing the mixture into molds has already been discussed, I feel the need to elaborate. The type of molds you choose is important as it can make or break your bath bombs. You don't want your finished product to crumble apart because you chose the wrong mold.

While there are many bath bomb molds out with intricate shapes and sizes, it is important to note that the simpler the mold the better. The problem with intricate molds is that if you are still new to crafting your bath bombs, you might not have the skills to pack them properly.

Clear plastic round molds and clam shells are quite common and practical. If you are a newbie, you can opt for these molds because they produce sturdy bath bombs that are perfectly constructed even if you haven't perfected packing the mixture into molds.

Ideally, molds should have a top and bottom part to allow for easy molding and demolding. This also gives bath bombs a finished and professional look. This is especially helpful if you are going to give the bath bombs away as presents to loved ones.

When stuffing molds with bath bomb mixtures, make sure you pack the mold firmly so there are no air spaces within the mixture. The presence of air pockets can affect the integrity of the bath bomb making it less sturdy and more likely to crumble.

Proper Storage

Bath bombs react to whatever moisture is available. Thus, they require a very dry climate as moisture in the air can cause them to prematurely fizz. However, this does not mean that you cannot use them if you live in a humid climate. You will just have to pay more attention to proper storage.

The best way to store bath bombs is inside airtight containers to protect from excess moisture in the air. Make sure the glass jars have a rubber seal on them to ensure that moisture cannot enter. You can also wrap them in plastic to seal them off from moisture. Another tip to remove excess moisture from the jar is to put a pack of silica gel in the container.

Aside from moisture, heat is another factor that can negatively affect bath bombs. Make sure you store them in places that are not near a heat source. The pantry or the bathroom closet are both great places to keep them.

Light can cause discoloration to bath bombs if they are exposed to too much of it. It is crucial to put them in a dark and dry place so their color remains brilliant for a long time. If you do not have a dark wooden box or a pantry and all you have is a transparent container, covering a glass jar with dark paper can also work.

You can also use a humidifier in the area where you store your bath bombs so they last longer without losing their fizz and scent.

Packaging

Whether you are making bath bombs for personal use or for your business, it is important that you not only know how to properly store them but also pack them. Bath bombs are made from ingredients that do not hold well together over time and they can fall apart and eventually make a mess. This is why it is important that you know how to pack them.

- **Wrap:** One of the most important things you can do is wrap them with cling wrap to hold their shape. You can also use parchment paper or a beautiful packaging paper to make them more interesting to look at.

- **Box:** Storing your bath bombs in wooden boxes is a good idea as you can easily take them out from storage when you need them. To protect them from breaking, line the interior of the box with a soft fabric.

- **Hang them:** Placing them in a bag and hanging them somewhere in your bathroom is a great way to store them, especially if space is an issue.

Tips and Tricks

Making bath bombs takes time and practice. Below are some important tips and tricks to avoid making mistakes and wasting precious ingredients:

- **A perfect bath bomb should not fizz while mixing the ingredients:** If you notice that your mixture is still puffing or fizzing even if you have thoroughly added all the wet ingredients, then it is too wet. If this happens, discard what you made and start over, using less water.

- **Add the right amount of wet ingredients:** The amount of wet ingredients you use depends on whether you live in a humid or dry area. If your area is humid, you don't need to add all wet ingredients. The texture of a good bath bomb is like wet sand, not dripping sand.

- **Use a warm oven to dry the bath bombs faster:** You can also dry the bath bombs in a warm oven. If you are using a muffin tray as your mold, heat the oven to 170^0F for ten minutes, then turn it off. Place the bath bombs inside with the oven door closed. Let them dry and they will be ready within eight hours.

- **Sift both citric acid powder and baking soda:** Before combining the two ingredients, sift them to remove the lumps. By doing so, you can ensure that the powders fuse together during the mixing process, so they will create large bubbles.

- **Use cornstarch for a smoother bath bomb:** Using cornstarch can help manage the fizzing reactions of the baking soda and citric acid powder so that once you drop it in water, it will not explode too much.

- **Always use cosmetic grade additives:** Additives like coloring and essential oil can cause reactions to the body. Only use cosmetic grade additives to ensure safety for the skin.

- **Use food grade baking soda:** There are two types of baking soda– food grade and industrial grade. Always opt for food grade because it is not as strong and does not contain any foreign matter that might result in an ugly or violent bath bomb.

- **Never use water when binding the dry ingredients:** Always avoid water when binding dry ingredients because it can cause an extreme fizzing reaction. This is why vegetable oil is used instead of water.

- **Use powdered coloring:** Powdered coloring does not add moisture to the bath bombs thus it does not contribute to the chemical reaction during the mixing process.

- **Make sure your molds are extremely dry:** The presence of even the tiniest amount of moisture on your molds can cause your mixture to fizz and ruin your bath bombs. It is crucial to make sure your molds are extremely dry before stuffing the mixture inside.

- **Cover the bath bombs with dry tissue paper:** While they are drying in the mold, cover the top of the bath bombs with dry tissue paper as this will absorb the moisture present in the air and the bath bombs.

- **Use witch hazel oil for faster drying:** Bath bombs made with witch hazel dry faster than those made with vegetable oil. So, if you need to make bath bombs urgently, use this oil.

- **Use your hands to mix all ingredients:** Using a wooden spoon will not ensure that all ingredients are mixed together.

Instead, use your hands. Just make sure you wear gloves as citric acid and baking powder can cause skin irritation.

- **Measure all ingredients correctly:** See to it that all ingredients are measured correctly so that the bath bomb mixture is neither too dry nor too wet.

- **Consume within a few weeks:** The bath bombs will lose their scent and fizz after a few weeks so make sure you use them immediately.

Troubleshooting

Despite following the tips and advice, you might still encounter problems when making bath bombs. This chapter will discuss troubleshooting so you know what to do if you encounter these situations.

- **Why does the bath bomb crumble when I take it out of the mold?** This is a common problem encountered by first-timers. They crumble because they are not firmly pressed into the mold or they are too dry. Before you pack it into molds, make sure the mixture has just enough moisture and that you press them firmly, such that there are no air spaces within them.

- **Why are they difficult to take out from the mold?** Bath bombs sticking to the mold is also a common occurrence. It means you have used too much water and cornstarch. To solve this problem, add citric acid and baking soda with a ratio of 1:2.

- **Why do my bath bombs easily flatten and soften?** This usually happens when you use too much water. To solve this problem, put the mixture back into a bowl and add baking soda. You can also add cornstarch, oatmeal or clay to make it less wet.

- **Why is my bath bomb just expanding into a blob and not fizzing up?** This happens when you add too much water during the mixing process. Remember that water can activate the reaction between the baking soda and citric acid, so too much of it can result in the premature release of effervescence. To remedy this, add two parts baking soda with one part citric acid.

- **Why are the ingredients not sticking together?** Simple. The ingredients are not sticking together because the mixture does not have enough moisture. Instead of adding water to make it damper, add witch hazel oil.

- **Why do my bath bombs crack once dried?** Bath bombs crack because they have too much water in them. Remember that water activates the reaction of baking soda and citric acid. This releases carbon dioxide from within the bombs, causing cracking.

Recipes

The best thing about making bath bombs is that you can personalize them according to what you want by experimenting and using different ingredients. When it comes to making bath bombs, there are hundreds of recipes you can try. This chapter will give you detailed steps on how to make various exciting bath bombs.

Basic Bath Bomb Recipe

Before you try any experimental bath bomb recipes, it is important that you master the basics so you can hone your confidence and eventually be successful with more advanced recipes.

Ingredients:

- 2 cups baking soda

- 1 cup citric acid

- 1 cup Epsom salt

- ½ teaspoon cosmetic grade coloring powder

- 1 drop essential oil of your choice

- a few drops witch hazel oil

Instructions:

1. In a dry, clean mixing bowl, combine the baking soda, citric acid and Epsom salt. Stir in the coloring powder.

2. Sift the dry ingredients to remove the lumps.

3. Add a drop of essential oil into the mixture, then mix using your glove-protected hands.

4. Place witch hazel oil in a spray bottle and spray a few times over the dry mixture. Mix vigorously and make sure that the

mixture is not too wet. It is advisable to spray it a few times then mix and test the moisture with your fingers.

5. Pack into molds and allow to dry for 1 to 2 days.

6. Place in air-tight glass jars.

Simple Aromatherapy Bath Bomb

This relaxing bath bomb recipe is infused with aromatic essential oil. This is also a great gift idea for friends and family.

Ingredients:

- 2 cups baking soda

- 1 cup citric acid

- 1 drop lavender essential oil

- 2 sprays witch hazel oil

Instructions:

1. Combine the baking soda and citric acid in a mixing bowl.

2. Sift through a sieve to remove the clumps.

3. Add a drop of lavender essential oil and mix using your hands. Wear gloves to protect your hands.

4. Place the witch hazel oil into a sprayer and mist the dry ingredients twice. Mix the ingredients and test the moisture with your fingers.

5. Pack firmly into molds and allow to dry for 24 hours or more.

6. Place in air-tight glass jars.

Glittery Easter Egg Bath Bomb

Make bath time fun for kids with this exciting Easter egg bath bomb recipe. The additional ingredients that you put in this bath bomb will surely make kids want to stay in the tub longer.

Ingredients:

- 1 tablespoon glitter

- 8 ounces Epsom salt

- 8 ounces cornstarch

- 8 ounces citric acid powder

- 8 ounces baking soda

- 1 tablespoon water

- 4 tablespoons essential oil

- 6 tablespoons almond oil

Instructions:

1. In a clean bowl, combine the glitter, Epsom salt, cornstarch, citric acid powder and baking soda. Mix until well combined.

2. Place in a spray bottle the water, essential oil and almond oil. Give a good shake.

3. Gradually spray the liquid into the dry ingredients until wet.

4. Wear gloves and mix the entire ingredients, working fast.

5. Pack the mixture into a silicone Easter egg mold and leave overnight until hard.

6. Take from the silicone mold and place in an air-tight container for storage.

Elegant Bath Bombs with Sugar Flower

This luxurious bath bomb recipe looks good enough to eat because it uses sugar flowers. While it is completely inedible, it looks very dainty thus making it a great gift for friends and family.

Ingredients:

- 4 ounces Epsom salt

- 4 ounces cornstarch

- 4 ounces citric acid

- 8 ounces baking soda

- A dash of powdered coloring

- 2 teaspoons peppermint essential oil

- ¾ teaspoon water

- 2 ½ teaspoons almond oil

- 1 tablespoon small sugar flowers

Instructions:

1. In a mixing bowl, combine the Epsom salt, cornstarch, citric acid, baking soda and powder coloring.

2. Sift the dry ingredients through a sieve to remove the lumps.

3. In a spray bottle, combine the essential oil, water and almond oil.

4. Spray the wet ingredients into the dry ingredients gradually. Mix until well combined, using gloved hands.

5. Once the right moisture is achieved, add in the sugar flowers. Mix.

6. Press into silicone molds.

7. Cover the top with a towel and allow to dry for at least 24 hours.

8. Once dried, place in an air-tight container until ready to use.

Messy Bath Bombs with Dried Flowers

As the name implies, this bath bomb can be messy because it contains dried flowers or herbs. Nevertheless, the dried flowers floating in the tub can create a relaxed feeling.

Ingredients:

- 6 ounces Epsom salt

- 6 ounces cornstarch

- 6 ounces citric acid

- 10 ounces baking soda

- A dash of coloring powder

- 4 teaspoons extra virgin olive oil

- 4 teaspoons essential oil

- 1 teaspoon water

- Dried flower and herbs

Instructions:

1. In a mixing bowl, combine the Epsom salt, cornstarch, citric acid, baking soda and powder coloring.

2. Sift the dry ingredients through a sieve to remove the lumps.

3. In a spray bottle, combine the essential oil, water and almond oil.

4. Spray the wet ingredients into the dry ingredients gradually. Mix until well combined using gloved hands.

5. Once the right moisture is achieved, add in the dried flowers.

6. Pack into silicone molds and place a towel on top.

7. Allow to dry for 48 hours.

8. Store in an air-tight container once dry.

Milky White Bath Bombs

This recipe is designed to make your skin soft and smooth. This recipe is for advanced bath bomb DIYers.

Ingredients:

- 1/3 cup powdered milk

- ½ cup cornstarch

- ¼ cup sea salt

- ¾ cup citric acid powder

- 1 cup baking soda

- 1 tablespoon grapeseed oil

- 1 tablespoon almond oil

- 1 tablespoon shea butter

- 1 tablespoon cocoa butter

Instructions:

1. In a dry mixing bowl, combine the milk powder, cornstarch, sea salt, citric acid and baking soda.

2. In a microwave-safe bowl, combine the grapeseed oil, almond butter, shea butter and cocoa butter. Microwave in 30-second increments until all ingredients melt.

3. Gradually pour the melted oil into the dry mixture.

4. Mix together using your gloved hand until everything is blended.

5. Once the right mixture is achieved, pack into silicone molds.

6. Allow to completely dry for 24 hours before storing into an air-tight container.

Salty Champagne Bath Bombs

Although this bath bomb recipe does not contain any champagne, it still relaxes you as though you are drinking champagne while soaking in the tub.

Instructions:

- 9 ounces baking soda

- 4 ounces citric acid powder

- 4 ounces cornstarch

- 4 ounces dead sea salt or Himalayan pink salt

- A dash of powdered coloring

- 2 teaspoons essential oil of your choice

- 2 ½ tablespoon vegetable oil

Instructions:

1. Combine the dry ingredients (baking soda, citric acid powder, cornstarch, salt and powdered coloring) in a mixing bowl.

2. Sift the dry ingredients to remove the lumps.

3. In another bowl, combine the essential oil and vegetable oil.

4. Add the oils gradually into the dry mixture and blend all ingredients using your hands. Make sure that you wear gloves while mixing everything.

5. Pack into hollow Christmas balls or other molds that you have available.

6. Allow to harden for two days before storing in an air-tight container.

Oatmilk Bath Bombs

This oatmeal and milk bath bomb recipe is great for exfoliating the skin. While the ingredients are different from the basic bath bomb recipe, making this recipe is very easy.

Ingredients:

- 1 tablespoons milk powder
- 3 tablespoons oatmeal
- 3 tablespoons Epsom salt
- 2 cups baking soda
- 1 cup citric acid
- Witch hazel oil (adjusted according to moisture needs)

Ingredients:

1. Mix the milk powder, oatmeal, salt, baking soda and citric acid in a bowl.
2. Gradually add drops of witch hazel oil to the dry ingredients.
3. Mix using your hands. Wear gloves to protect your hands.
4. Place into molds and allow to dry for 48 hours.
5. Place in an air-tight container once dry for storage.

Ylang Butter Bath Bombs

This aromatic bath bomb can help you relax as well as benefit from softer skin because of its unique ingredients.

Ingredients:

- ½ cup citric acid powder

- 1 cup baking soda

- 5 drops ylang essential oil

- 2 drops musk fragrance oil

- ½ cup cocoa butter, grated

- Witch hazel oil

Instructions:

1. In a mixing bowl, mix together the citric acid and baking soda.

2. Sift both ingredients through a sieve to remove any clumps.

3. Gradually stir in the essential oil, musk and cocoa butter.

4. Mix until well combined. If the mixture is too dry, spray with witch hazel oil.

5. Press into molds and allow to dry for 48 hours.

6. Store in a cool, dry place inside an air-tight container.

Milky and Floral Bath Bombs

This milky bath bomb is made more luxurious with the addition of dried petals. It is a simple recipe that yields an upscale result.

Ingredients:

- ¼ cup powdered milk

- ½ cup citric acid powder

- 1 cup baking soda

- 1/3 cup Epsom salt

- 7 teaspoons witch hazel oil

- 1 teaspoon essential oil of your choice

- 2 teaspoons cocoa butter, melted

- 2 tablespoon olive oil

- 1 teaspoon dried calendula leaves

Instructions:

1. In a mixing bowl, mix together the milk, citric acid powder and baking soda.

2. Sift to remove the lumps.

3. Add in the Epsom salt.

4. In a sprayer, combine the witch hazel oil, essential oil, cocoa butter and olive oil.

5. Spray the oil mixture into dry ingredients.

6. Add in the dried calendula flowers.

7. Combine the mixture using a wooden spoon or with your gloved hands.

8. Test the mixture continuously.

9. Pack into the mold and press firmly. Then allow to dry for 48 hours.

10. Store in an air-tight container.

Salty Oats Bath Bombs

This bath bomb recipe contains oatmeal and Epsom salt, ingredients that not only make you feel relaxed but also exfoliate your skin.

Ingredients:

- ¼ cups citric acid
- 1 cup baking soda
- ½ cup ground oatmeal
- ½ cup Epsom salt
- A dash of powdered coloring
- 2 tablespoons witch hazel oil
- 1 teaspoon essential oil of your choice
- 4 tablespoons coconut oil

Ingredients:

1. In a mixing bowl, combine the citric acid and baking soda.
2. Sift to remove the lumps.
3. Place back into the mixing bowl and add the oatmeal, Epsom salt and powdered coloring.
4. In a smaller bowl, combine the witch hazel oil, essential oil and coconut oil.

5. Use a dropper and gradually add the wet ingredients to the dry ingredients.

6. Wear gloves and use your hands to mix the entire mixture.

7. Make sure that it has the right amount of moisture before packing into the molds.

8. Allow to dry for 48 hours.

9. Store in an air-tight container.

Apricot Bath Bombs

With its fruity smell and oatmeal, this apricot bath bomb does not only have an exciting aroma, it can also help exfoliate for smooth skin.

Ingredients:

- 2 tablespoons cornstarch

- ¼ cup baking soda

- 2 tablespoons citric acid

- A dash of coloring powder

- ¼ cup oatmeal

- 10 drops essential oil of your choice

- 1 tablespoon witch hazel oil

- 1 ½ tablespoon apricot oil

Instructions:

1. In a mixing bowl, combine the cornstarch, baking soda and citric acid.

2. Sift to remove the lumps.

3. Add the coloring powder and oatmeal. Mix until well-combined.

4. In a smaller bowl, mix together the essential oil, witch hazel oil and apricot oil.

5. Use a medicine dropper and add the wet ingredients gradually.

6. With gloved hands, combine all ingredients and make sure to test the moisture.

7. If the right moisture is achieved, pack into molds.

8. Allow to dry for 24-48 hours.

9. Store in air-tight containers.

Muscle Relief Bath Bombs

This particular recipe contains ingredients that will help soothe your tired and aching muscles. You will definitely want to soak in the tub a little longer.

Ingredients:

- ½ cup baking soda

- 1/3 cup Epsom salts

- 2 tablespoons cream of tartar

- ½ teaspoon fresh rosemary, chopped

- 2 tablespoons coconut oil, melted

- 1 teaspoon peppermint oil

- Witch hazel oil

Instructions:

1. Combine the baking soda, Epsom salt and cream of tartar into a mixing bowl. Stir in chopped rosemary.

2. Gradually stir in the coconut oil and peppermint oil.

3. Adjust the moisture by adding drops of witch hazel oil slowly.

4. Mix with your gloved hands.

5. Press the mixture into ice cube trays or other bath bomb molds that you have.

6. Allow to set for 24 hours in a cool and dry area.

7. Store in air-tight containers or use immediately.

Spinning Bath Bombs

Spinning bath bombs are very fun to watch. They are made from the same ingredients used for basic bath bombs. The only difference is that they spin like crazy and they give you the best fizz ever!

Ingredients:

- 1 cup citric acid powder

- 2 cups baking soda

- ½ cup cornstarch

- ½ cup Epsom salt

- ¼ teaspoon powdered coloring

- 20 to 25 drops lavender oil

- 3 tablespoons sweet almond oil

- Witch hazel oil mixed with equal parts 91% alcohol

Instructions:

1. In a mixing bowl, mix the citric acid, baking soda, cornstarch and Epsom salt. Add in the powdered coloring.

2. Pour gradually the lavender oil and almond oil.

3. Use your hands to mix everything. Be sure to wear gloves before mixing the ingredients.

4. Place the witch hazel oil and alcohol mixture in a spray bottle.

5. Gradually mist the bath bomb mixture with the witch hazel oil mixture until you achieve the right moisture level.

6. Pack the mixture into molds and gently tap to remove the bath bomb. Set the bath bombs on a piece of cardboard or wax paper.

7. Allow to dry for at least 24 hours before storing in airtight containers.

Lemon Vanilla Bath Bombs

Fresh citrus combined with vanilla can give you a very pleasant and comforting bath experience.

Ingredients:

- 1 cup baking soda

- ½ cup citric acid

- ½ cup cornstarch

- 3 tablespoons Epsom salts

- 2 teaspoon coconut oil

- 15 drops lemon essential oil

- ½ teaspoon vanilla

- 4 tablespoons dried lemon zest

- Witch hazel oil

Instructions

1. In a mixing bowl, combine the baking soda, citric acid, cornstarch and Epsom salt.

2. Add gradually the coconut oil, essential oil, vanilla and lemon zest.

3. Wear gloves and use your hands to mix all the ingredients.

4. Gradually add drops of witch hazel oil to adjust the moisture. Use your hands to mix everything.

5. Once it is moist enough, pack into bath bombs and allow to dry for at least 24 hours.

6. Store in an air tight container or use immediately.

Coconut Oil Bath Bombs

Coconut oil has great moisturizing qualities and using it in bath bombs will improve your skin quality.

Ingredients:

- 1 cup baking soda

- ¼ cup citric acid

- ½ cup cornstarch

- ½ cup Epsom salt

- 3 tablespoons coconut oil

- 1 teaspoon almond oil

- Witch hazel oil

Instructions:

1. In a mixing bowl, combine the soda, citric acid, cornstarch and Epsom salt.

2. Stir in the coconut oil and almond oil.

3. Wear gloves and use your hands to mix everything.

4. Gradually add witch hazel oil to adjust the moisture.

5. Pack into molds and allow to dry for 48 hours.

6. Store in air-tight containers.

Lavender Honey Donut Bath Bombs

This bath bomb looks (and smells) delicious enough to eat! Even though you cannot eat these, they do make your bath time relaxing and fun.

Ingredients:

- 1 cup baking soda

- ½ cup citric acid

- ½ cup Epsom salt

- ½ cup cornstarch

- 2 teaspoon lavender essential oil

- 2 tablespoons coconut oil

- A few drops of food coloring

- Witch hazel oil

- ½ pound white melting soap

- Colored sprinkles

Instructions:

1. In a mixing bowl, combine the dry ingredients – baking soda, citric acid, Epsom salt and cornstarch.

2. Add the essential oil, coconut oil and food coloring.

3. Use a gloved hand to mix all ingredients.

4. Gradually add witch hazel oil to adjust the moisture.

5. Pack the mixture into silicone donut molds and allow to dry for 48 hours.

6. Take the bath bombs out and dip one side into melted soap and add colored sprinkles on top.

7. Allow to dry.

Continuing Education with More Advanced Techniques

Now that you have learned how to make easy bath bomb recipes, you are ready for more advanced techniques. There are several advanced techniques you can use to make your bath bombs more interesting and attractive. This chapter will discuss a few that you can try for your future projects.

Bath Bombs with Layers of Color

The best thing about making your own bath bombs is that you have the freedom to create the most colorful ones on the market. It is easy to make bath bombs that come with layers of color. Aside from your usual bath bomb ingredients, you need a few powdered colors you can mix to create layered effects.

Once you have created the base of the basic bath bomb, divide it into as many portions as colors that you want. Place in separate mixing bowls and add a small amount of your favorite color. Give the contents in each bowl a mix. Press one colored mixture into the mold firmly. Add the next layer of color. Continue adding layers until you are satisfied. The number of layers you are trying to achieve will dictate the thickness of each layer. Allow to dry for the usual 48 hours before storing them in air-tight containers.

Hide Something Inside

You can use bath bombs to hide small things inside. Using the basic bath bomb recipe or other any other recipe you want to use, hide small items like a small bath toy or compressed washcloth in the middle of the bath bomb. However, you will need a bigger mold so that the bath bomb ingredients will hold well together around the object, depending on the size.

Floating Bath Bombs

Bath bombs naturally sink but floating bath bomb projects have been circulating around the web lately. Contrary to what most people think, floating bath bombs are not made from special light materials. In fact, they are made from the same materials as your basic bath bombs.

What makes them float is that they are smaller than conventional bath bombs and they are loosely packed, thus making them more buoyant. Another way to make them float is to add more lightweight additives, such as cornstarch.

Lastly, the type of mold used can also make your bath bomb float. Instead of opting for the less buoyant sphere, use a flat mold with more surface area so that it can float on water.

Glitter bombs

Glitter bath bombs are a way to bring your daytime glam into the tub. You can turn most recipes into glitter bath bombs simply by including glitters and salt in the dry ingredients. As a bonus, it makes them look very expensive. When making this bath bomb, prepare to get messy. Glitter will most likely be found in your home (or hair or hands) for some time after crafting. But imagine how fun the result will be, especially for children.

Bubbling Bath Bombs

It is natural for bath bombs to fizz, but what if you could make them bubble? This is possible by using sodium lauryl sulfoacetate. Using your basic bath bomb recipe or another recipe that you have in mind, add 10% to 15% sodium lauryl sulfoacetate to your mix. For instance, if you are using 2 cups of baking soda and 1 cup of citric acid, you can add ½ cup of sodium lauryl sulfoacetate. You will also need to adjust the recipe further by adding more oil to make the mixture more moist.

If you are concerned about sodium lauryl sulfoacetate being an irritant, you will only be using a small amount of it. For safety purposes, wear safety goggles, a dust mask and gloves to protect yourself from exposure.

There are so many advanced techniques you can use when making bath bombs. Your only limit is your creativity! Following these tips will greatly help you improve your skills and techniques as well as make bath time more fun for you and your family.

Resources and Suppliers

Bath bomb ingredients are ubiquitous, and they are found in many grocery stores. But how do you know if you bought quality grade ingredients? Buying the ingredients to make bath bombs sounds easy but if you want the best results for your DIY bath bomb creations, it is crucial that you know how to buy the right ingredients. Below is a guide on where to get high grade ingredients to use in your bath bomb recipes.

Baking Soda

Did you know that there are different types of baking soda available on the market? How can you make sure you get the best baking soda for your bath bombs?

It is crucial that you always opt for food grade baking soda. Never skimp and buy animal grade or industrial grade baking soda often found in hardware stores. These types of baking soda likely come with inconsistent sizes of granules that may cause problems concerning unequal fizzing.

There are many local brands of baking soda that are great for making bath bombs. Baking brands of sodium bicarbonate are best because they have the same consistency and size.

I recommend ARM & HAMMER because it has the most consistent particle size compared to other brands. If you cannot find this brand in your local grocery or baking store, you can always look for it online. You can also try other brands that are available but make sure that you experiment first to find out if the brand works for you.

Citric Acid

Citric acid is derived from natural acids occurring in fruits and vegetables. It is not only used for cooking, but also for making personal care products. When sourcing the citric acid that you are going to use for making bath bombs, there are a few factors you need to consider.

- **Where is it sourced from?** Determine where your citric acid comes from. If it is sourced from abroad, there is a possibility that it will have lower quality because it is exposed to different elements. Try to find a citric acid powder that is made locally.

- **When was it manufactured?** It is important to determine when the citric acid powder was made. The older the citric acid powder is, the more unreliable it is. Citric acid hardens over time, which will eventually make it unusable. Thus, it is important that you buy the newest and freshest materials to make sure they will not affect your bath bombs.

- **Is it too large or too small?** The particle size of citric acid can make a huge difference in the bath bombs. Citric acid particles should be of an adequate size, about the size of iodized salt, to react properly with the baking soda.

When it comes to finding the right brand of citric acid for making bath bombs, it is up to you to decide. You can shop for it in your local grocery store, but if you struggle to find it, it is available online. Be sure to check reviews before you purchase.

Essential Oils

Essential oils give bath bombs aromas and extra therapeutic benefits. When buying essential oils for your bath bombs, make sure you test them first. Visit stores that sell a wide variety of essential oils and use the available testers to choose which ones you prefer in your bath bombs.

It is important to opt for high-quality essential oils instead of the cheap imitation oils because they might have some negative effects on the body. Therefore, it is important that you buy from local natural food stores that sell real essential oils. Try brands like Doterra and Young Living, as they are both true and certified essential oil brands.

Certified essential oils can cost a lot of money, so it is wise to invest in the type of essential oils that you will likely love and use a lot. You can also buy wholesale essential oils, especially if you are planning to make bath bombs regularly or in bulk.

Salts

Always opt for either Epsom salt, sea salt or bath salts when making bath bombs. You can buy them in health stores and drug stores. Both Epsom and sea salts are cheaper compared to bath salts. If you're making your first bath bomb or are testing out a new recipe, you can opt to use the cheaper types of salts. Avoid using cooking salt. Cooking salts such as iodized salt dry out skin and should not be used.

Color

Coloring is an important ingredient when making bath bombs. They make the finished product stand out beautifully. When choosing coloring agents, use food grade powdered colors because they will dissolve in water the most effectively.

There are many synthetic dyes you can get from baking supply shops but the problem with synthetic coloring is that they also color the water and eventually stick to the sides of the tub, thereby staining it. If you want to choose a more natural and organic coloring, you can use powdered mica. Mica is a natural mineral that produces nice, soft colors and it does not color the water.

Finding powdered mica can be difficult, as you cannot buy it from ordinary grocery stores. However, there are many online stores that sell good quality powdered mica you can use to create your bath bombs.

Surfactants

Surfactants are used in bath bombs to produce bubbles and foam. Below are some examples of foaming surfactants.

- **Sodium lauryl sulfate powder:** Also known as SLS powder, this surfactant is used to make all kinds of foaming products. It is a popular ingredient for making shampoos and body washes. If you want to use this material, find a supplier that sells highly concentrated powder of at least 80% so you can get the best value for your money. But before you use them, make sure you test them on your skin because they can cause irritation.

- **Sodium cocoyl isethionate:** A new generation of surfactants, this is a good alternative to SLS. However, you may need to heat this ingredient before blending it into the bath bomb mixture.

- **Sodium lauryl sulfoacetate:** This surfactant comes in different forms–powder, flake and coarse. Coarse sodium lauryl sulfoacetate is popularly used in bath bombs. The best thing about this ingredient is that it is biodegradable and eco-friendly, making it a great option for sustainable bath bombs.

- **Coco glucoside:** This type of surfactant produces long-lasting foam. Aside from bath bombs, it is also found in most facial cleansers, shampoos and bath products.

Surfactants are a bit challenging to find. You cannot buy them from grocery stores or beauty shops because they are industrial ingredients. The best way to buy them is online. When buying surfactants, make sure you research their quality and the company you are buying them from.

Conclusion

Bath bombs are simple bath time essentials that allow you to have fun while taking a bath. While there are many shops that sell various types of bath bombs, there is nothing more rewarding than creating your very own. Making your own bath bombs is easy and only requires simple, easily available ingredients. Once you perfect the craft, you will be able to make bath time fun and relaxing. The best thing about making your own bath bombs is that you know what goes into them so you can ensure that the ingredients are friendly to your unique skin. Making bath bombs is a simple process that anyone–even a DIY newbie–can do. It is a fun project you can enjoy and share with the rest of your family and friends. We hope that we inspired you to get crafting, regardless of your skill level.

If you've enjoyed reading this book, subscribe* to my mailing list for exclusive content and sneak peaks of my future books

Go to the link below:

http://eepurl.com/dClyGl

OR

Use the QR Code:

(*Must be 13 years or older to subscribe)